Butterfly Made Easy
for Southwest Florida

A Guide to Attracting and Keeping
Butterflies in Your Garden

Tiger Swallowtail
(Papilio glaucus)

MIKE MALLOY

To order additional copies, please contact us.
BookSurge, LLC
www.booksurge.com
1-866-308-6235
orders@booksurge.com

Interior book formatting and cover design by
Rend Graphics || www.rendgraphics.com

Acknowledgments

I would like to thank the following people, for their time, effort, conversations and encouragement.

Dr. Doug Caldwell, Entomologist, University of Florida IFAS Extension, Collier County, Florida

Dr. Jan Abernathy, Director of Horticulture, Naples Zoo and Caribbean Gardens

Ken Werner, owner of Gulf Coast Butterflies

Carol Sweat, Collier County Master Gardener

Chuck Ray, Collier County Master Gardener

Renee Jones, Collier County Master Gardener

Kevin Sullivan, my long-time friend, who introduced me to gardening some forty years ago.

I would like to add a special thanks to all the butterflies of the world for giving me the opportunity to admire their physical beauty and mesmerizing flight, for they are the stars of this book, and to all the people who care about them and their conservation.

Most importantly, I would like to thank Cathleen Feser, Urban Horticulture Extension Educator, Collier County, Florida, for her sense of humor, time and valuable assistance in helping me put this book together.

Dedication

First and foremost, this book is dedicated to my wife Jackie, who has loved and stood by me for the past thirty years through my addiction to butterflies, and to Nash and Perry who have kept me company for hours on end while 'butterflying'.

If a man was to have it all, it would be me.

Table of Contents

Introduction

This book was designed to give you practical and easy tips for attracting and keeping butterflies in your Southwest Florida garden.

Much of the butterfly's natural habitat has been destroyed by urbanization. Butterfly gardening is not only a great way to observe the beauty of these creatures; it can also contribute to their conservation. This book will help you recognize your common local butterflies, and help identify what plants to install to attract and keep them in your yard. As for location of the plants, there should at least four hours of sun, but there are some butterflies that prefer shaded areas so having both areas is ideal. A good watering system is also important for both plant growth and caterpillar protection. Sprinkler heads used for lawns are too forceful, and can blow new larvae off the host plants in addition to shredding the flowers. I use soaker hoses or micro sprinklers (low pressure systems).

A viewing area is a must to watch the butterflies unique and various habits. For example, the Monarch is a very territorial butterfly, and will chase off any unwanted intruders in his territory. I have actually seen them chase birds out of 'their' areas. Butterflies have no way of doing harm to other creatures. They have no weapons, and usually, the larger and faster butterfly wins these 'district' disputes. Another example is the female Sulfur, who will circle skyward with the male in chase during the mating ritual. This is truly something to see.

Watching female butterflies choosing the plants on which to deposit their eggs is fascinating. First, they taste the plant with their feet to be sure it is the right plant that will feed the larvae when it emerges from the egg. 'Puddling' is another great ritual to observe. When puddling, groups of butterflies will congregate on the ground using their proboscis (tongues) to draw minerals, salts, and water from the ground. Butterflies are cold-blooded, and therefore need sun and warmth to heat up their bodies enough to fly. On some cloudy and cool days butterflies will sometimes stay in the same spot all day. Basking in the sun is one of the surest ways to observe butterflies in a motionless state. Some have their wings flattened out; others will keep their wings closed in an upright position, while still other butterflies will actually tilt one wing to get the most out of the sun's energy.

I have also attracted hummingbirds to my garden because some of the plants used to attract butterflies also attract hummingbirds. Fire Bush, Fire Spike, and Cigar Plant are just a few examples. Ideally, there should be some shrubs and trees around the perimeter of your butterfly garden to give butterflies a place to rest, hide from predators, get out of the rain, and roost at night.

Butterfly Facts *and* Biology

Species
There are 760 butterfly species in North America and at least 100 of those species can be found in Florida. There are another 70 species known as Skippers. Skippers have stouter bodies and shorter wings than 'regular' butterflies.   Butterflies and skippers have very slender, wire-like antennae with club-like appendages on the tips.   In contrast, moths have wide, feathery antennae and are far less flamboyant in color. They also have very stout bodies. Most moths are more active at night, while butterflies and skippers are day fliers. Moth's antennae are more sensitive than the butterfly's antennae for finding food in the dark. Both moths and butterflies are masters of camouflage, equipped with eyespots on their wings and bright colors to ward off predators.

Life Cycle
The butterfly undergoes complete metamorphosis, which means it has four stages of life: egg, larva, pupa, and adult. Butterflies lay their eggs on specific plants known as 'host plants'. Within a few days, the caterpillars emerge and begin to devour the host plant. This is the second, or larva, stage. Caterpillars have enormous appetites and can grow at an astonishing rate. As they grow, they shed their skin (molt) several times. Each skin-shedding process is known as an 'instar' and caterpillars can have four or five instars in their lives. Once fully grown, the caterpillar will seek a safe place to enter the third, or pupa, stage.   Prior to entering the pupa stage, the caterpillars begin to wander around as if they were lost. Ultimately, they will find the 'right' spot, where the caterpillar will shed its skin for the last time and form a chrysalis. The chrysalis is a cocoon-like structure where the final stage of metamorphosis occurs, and the caterpillar emerges as a beautiful adult butterfly. Butterflies in the adult form do not spread disease or harm anything. They are simply there for us to admire.

Butterflies *for* Florida Gardens

Painted Lady
Vanessa cardui

Zebra Longwing
Heliconius charitonius

Host Plants:
Passion Vines: Maypop (*Passiflora incarnata*)
Corkey-Stemmed (*Passiflora suberosa*)
Incense (*Passiflora incense*)

The Zebra Longwing is the state butterfly and abundant in southwest Florida. They are often called the 'social' butterflies due to their unique habit of going out on their own during the day and coming back to roost with the same group, sometimes twenty or thirty, in the same place every night. Zebra Longwings are one of the very few butterflies that actually collect pollen and it is thought this activity is the reason many can live up to six months. Be sure to plant your passion vines in shade or semi shade for Zebra Longwings.

Description:
Black with yellow stripes on the wings; rosy-red patch on the underside of hind wings.

Caterpillars:
White with black spines.

Field Notes:

Palamedes Swallowtail
Papilio palamedes

Host Plants:
Sweet Bay Magnolia (*Magnolia virginiana*)

The Palamedes Swallowtail is one of the showiest butterflies in southwest Florida.

Description:
Black and bright yellow; black stripes on fore wings; two blue eyespots on lower hind wings; pointed tails on hind wings; females may be solid Black.

Caterpillar:
Looks like bird droppings; two eyespots on the front of body;

Field Notes:

Queen
Danaua gilippus

Host Plants:
Scarlet Milkweed (*Asclepias curassavica*)

The Queen butterfly is a year round resident, but most abundant in southwest Florida in late Spring and Summer through early Fall. Males have scent pouches to attract females. The pouches are visible as a brownish blotch on the hind wings.

Description:
Rusty honey-brown; fore and hind wings outlined in black; fore wings speckled with white; males have brownish blotches near inner margins of hind wings.

Caterpillars:
Black, yellow, gray and white multi-colored stripes; three sets of tubercles.

Field Notes:

Monarch
Danaus plexippus

Host Plant:
Scarlet Milkweed (*Asclepias curassavica*)
Swamp Milkweed (*Asclepias perennis*)
Butterfly Weed (*Asclepias tuberosa*)

The Monarch is the most easily recognized butterfly in the world. Although the Monarch is abundant in southwest Florida year round, in winter the monarch migrates from other parts of the country to the state of Michoacan in Mexico. Males have scent pouches on their hind wings, which are used to attract female butterflies.

Description:
Orange-brown, fore and hind wings margins ringed in black, speckled with white; distinctive black 'veins' on fore and hind wings .

Caterpillar:
Black yellow, green white multi-colored stripes; two sets of tubercles, one set on the head, and one set at the rear of its body.

Field Notes:

Gulf Fritillary
Agraulis vanillae nigrior

Host Plants:
Passion Vines: Maypop (*Passiflora incarnata*)
Corkey-Stemmed (*Passiflora suberosa*)
Incense (*Passiflora incense*)

The Gulf Fritillary is abundant in Southwest Florida and therefore easy to attract. The Gulf Fritillary is a fast flying sun lover.

Description:
Bright orange with black spots on its fore and hind wings; aluminum foil-like patches on the underside of the fore and hind wings.

Caterpillar:
Black with rusty orange colored stripes along the sides; soft black spines running the full length of its body.

Field Notes:

Cloudless Sulfur
Phoebis sennae eubule

Host Plants:
Cassias (Senna species)

Cloudless Sulfurs are migratory and abundant in Florida during spring, summer and fall.

Description:
Pale yellow to lime-green; some fore wing margins dotted with brown; single brown eyespot in center of each fore wing.

Caterpillar:
Green with yellow stripe on each side.

Field Notes:

Buckeye
Junonia coenia

Host Plants:
Frogfruit (*Lippia nodiflora*)
Water Hyssop (*Bacopa monnieri*)

The Buckeye is abundant in Southwest Florida in the spring and summer. Some Buckeyes migrate north in the summer and back south in the winter. The very showy oscelli make the Buckeye appear larger than it actually is and are very effective in confusing predators.

Description:
Dull brownish-orange with multi-colored oscelli on the fore and hind wings; wavy cream and gold stripes along lower edge of hind wings.

Caterpillar:
Black with two orange stripes on sides; entire body covered with spines.

Field Notes:

Eastern Black Swallowtail
Papilio polyxenes

Host Plants:
Parsley (*Petroselinum crispum*)
Dill (*Anethum graveolens*)
Fennel (*Foeniculum vulgare*)

The Black Swallowtail is a very lofty flyer and abundant in southwest Florida in the spring and summer. The bright orange oscelli is used to distract predators from the main body parts.

Description:
Bluish-black color with two rows of yellow splashes along the margins of fore and hind wings; club-like extensions (tails) on lower margins of hind wings; blue color on hind wings is brighter on the female.

Caterpillar:
Green with black, orange and white spots on each side of its body. The caterpillars also have the defense mechanism of osmeteria, horn-like tubes that emit a foul odor to ward off predators.

Field Notes:

Gold Rim
Battus polydamas lucayus

Host Plants:
Dutchman's Pipe (*Aristolochia elegans*)
(*Aristolochia gigantean*)

The Gold Rim is the only swallowtail that does not have tails on its hind wings, thus making it easy to spot. Abundant in southwest Florida in spring, summer and early fall, Gold Rim's are lazy flyers, but when disturbed will bolt off rapidly.

Description:
Black with yellow bands on the lower margins of fore and hind wings; bluish markings on top of fore wings.

Caterpillar:
Rusty brown; two yellow osmeteria which emit a foul odor to ward off any predators.

Field Notes:

Malachite
Siproeta stelenes biplagiata

Host Plants:
Green Shrimp Plant (*Blechum brownie*)

The Malachite is a rare sight in Southwest Florida. Although the Malachite has a small tail on the margin of each hind wing, it is not a member of the Swallowtail group of butterflies. The color and markings of the Malachite resemble stained glass and make this butterfly one of the most outstanding of its species.

Description:
Electric green color; scalloped edges on fore and hind wings; blackish brown with green blotches on fore and hind wings; green spots on the hind wing margins.

Caterpillar: Black with orange spines.

Field Notes:

Painted Lady
Vanessa virginiensis

Host Plants:
Thistles (*Cirsium horridulum*)

Second only to the Monarch in migrational habits and abundancy, the Painted Lady is a quick flyer and travels from Mexico to Canada.

Description:
Orange-brown with white spots on fore wings.

Caterpillar:
Small, dull brown

Field Notes:

Southern White
Ascia monuste phileta

Host Plants:
Pepper Grass (*Lepidium virginicum*)

The Southern White is a fast erratic flyer and one of the most abundant butterflies in southwest Florida.

Description:
Males are almost pure white; the females hind and fore wings margins are lined in brown; underside sometimes pale yellow.

Caterpillar:
Yellow and green stripes with raised black bumps running laterally down their sides; clubs on the tip of antennae are a beautiful sky blue.

Field Notes:

White Peacock
Anartia jatrophe

Host Plants:
Water Hassop (*Bacopa monnieri*)
Frog Fruit (*Lippa nodifloria*)

The White Peacock is one of Florida's most beautiful butterflies. It is pearly white with yellow-orange margins. The peacock has a very fast and darting style of flight. Common in open fields and along waters edges were its host plants are found. Can be seen in southwest Florida year round, but more abundant in spring and summer.

Description:
Two large eyespots on the fore wings; two smaller eyespots on hind wings.

Caterpillar:
Small, black; very difficult to find.

Field Notes:

Viceroy
Basilarchia archippus floridensis

Host Plants:
Carolina Willow *(Salix caroliniana)*

The Viceroy is found in wet areas where it's host plant thrives. Abundant in Florida Spring , Summer and Fall.

Description:
Deep rust color with white spots on hind and fore wings, along the black margins. Well defined black veins running through both hind and fore wings.

Caterpillar:
Resembles a bird dropping with a large pair of horns in the head area.

Field Notes:

Red Admiral
Vanessa atalanta rubria

Host Plants:
False Nettle (*Boehmeria cylindrica*)
Burning Nettle (*Urtica urens*)

The Red Admiral is a beautiful butterfly. Like the Painted Lady, the Red Admiral is abundant in southwest Florida and throughout the world. The under side of the Red Admiral's wings are a completely different color and pattern than the upper side, which provides a effective camouflage from predators, particularly while in flight. The caterpillar has a creative method of weaving silk around leaf edges on the host plant, forming a 'nest' to rest and hide from predators during the day.

Description:
Black color; margins of hind wings are reddish-orange; fore wings have central reddish-orange bands; fore wing tips are speckled with white.

Caterpillar:
Black and white speckled; feeds at night.

Field Notes:

Orange Barred Sulfur
Phoebis philea

Host Plants:
Bahama Senna (*Cassia bicapsularis*)
Desert Senna (*Cassia nemorphila*)

The Orange Barred Sulfur is one of the largest, most colorful butterflies in Southwest Florida and is abundant year round. I have found that the Bahama Senna (*Cassia bicapsularis*) is their favorite host plant. Orange Barred Sulfurs are fast flyers, and have been referred to as the acrobats of the butterfly world.

Description:
Females are yellow in spring and summer; in fall and winter the color changes to a deeper yellow with orange patches on the hind wings; males are bright yellow year round with orange patches on the fore and hind wings.

Caterpillars:
Yellow, light and dark green stripes.

Field Notes:

Julia
Dryas iulia largo

Host Plants:
Passion Vines: Maypop (*Passiflora incaranata*)
Corkey-Stemmed (*Passiflora suberosa*)
Incense (*Passiflora incense*)

The Julia butterfly is a very fast flying sun lover. The Julia's long wing span makes this very fast flyer fun to watch. This butterfly is abundant in Southwest Florida during spring, summer and fall. The front legs are used to taste the leaves of the host plant, ensuring the eggs are laid on the correct plant, and that when the eggs hatch the caterpillars have the right food and enough of it to sustain them through this stage of their lives.

Description:
Males are brilliant orange; females have a duller orange color with wavy brown stripes on outer margins of fore and hind wings.

Caterpillar:
Chocolate brown with white spots over entire body; soft black spines run the entire length of its back.

Field Notes:

Giant Swallowtail
Heraclides cresphontes

Host Plants:
Wild Lime (*Zanthoxylum fagara*)
Citrus

The Giant Swallowtail is the largest of southwest Florida's swallowtails. A spectacular butterfly, Giant Swallowtails can have a wing span of up to six inches. The Swallowtail's flight is a graceful bobbing and floating motion, a thrill to watch as the butterfly bounces and floats to and from nectar flowers. Abundant in spring, summer, and fall where citrus is present. The eyespots and the yellow dot on the tails are effective in distracting predators.

Description:
Black with yellow spots running along the margins of fore and hind wings, yellow spotted stripe running across fore wings. The tails on its hind wings have a yellow dot on the tip, with two bluish-orange eyespots on the inner part of the hind wing.

Caterpillar:
Initially resembles brownish-white bird droppings, becoming grayish with maturity; red osmeteria, horn-like tubes which emit a foul odor to chase away any annoying predators.

Field Notes:

Sleepy Orange
Eurema nicippe

Host Plant:
Cassias (Coffee senna)

The Sleepy Orange is a beautiful butterfly about the size of your thumb nail. The beautiful yellow color of this butterfly reminds me of gold. The Sleepy Orange is abundant in southwest Florida in the spring and summer. Its flight is quick and erratic, and the butterflies are easy to spot, gathering in large numbers by the host plant. Sleepy Orange always sip nectar with their wings closed in an upright position.

Description:
Wings are golden yellow above, with brown markings on the margins of both fore and hind wings

Caterpillar: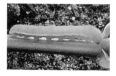
Lime Green with a white dash marks running down each side.

Field Notes:

Atala
Eumaeus atala florida

Host Plant:
Coontie (*Cycad* spp.)

The Atala is one of Florida's most spectacular butterflies. Only about two inches long, the Atala is a slow flier, and although this butterfly is found mostly on the east coast of Florida, I thought it was worth mentioning. Here in southwest Florida there has been an increased use of Coontie in municipal highway and urban plantings, and one can only hope the Atala will find its way here.

Description:
Metallic blue fore and hind wings; red abdomen; bluish dots along lower margin of hind wings.

Caterpillar:
Reddish color with yellow spots.

Field Notes:

Nectar Plants

Nectar Plants

When planting your butterfly garden remember to include both host plants, which will invite female butterflies to deposit their eggs, and nectar plants that will feed adult butterflies. If you have host and nectar plants, there is a good chance they will stay around after emerging from their chrysalis and your garden will have an abundance of butterflies for your viewing pleasure. Planting both host and nectar plants in groupings instead of one here and one there is the best way to encourage butterflies to remain close to 'home'. If you have what will sustain them, most butterflies will not travel far from were they are born. Butterflies will see a mass of their favorite color easier and cruising butterflies will most likely stop and take up residence.

I found butterflies prefer red, yellow and lavender flowers most. But I have seen them on white, blue and other colored flowers. The white flowers will also help to attract moths at night . I planted my host plants with masses of nectar plants surrounding them so when you are successful and the caterpillars eat them down, the plants will not be unsightly as they grow back. A sunny location is preferred but semi shade is also important, so try planting in both locations. Planting a perimeter of evergreens around your garden will help shelter and protect butterflies in bad weather, provide a spot for roosting at night or in the heat of the day, or when they just want to rest.

Amending the soil in your butterfly garden is usually not necessary. Group your plants according to water requirements. Survey the wet and dry areas in your yard and plant accordingly. Dead-heading (removing spent flowers) will encourage more blooms. Florida has a year round butterfly season so plant nectar plants to bloom at different times of the year so butterflies have a continuous source of nectar. Have fun watching your new friends arrive.

Tropical Sage
Salvia coccinea
Full sun to partial shade
Low water

Porterweed
Stachytarphaeta urticifolia
Full sun to partial shade
Low water

Scorpion Tail
Heliotropium angiospermum
Full sun to light shade
Low water

Beach Sunflower
Helianthus debilis
Full sun
Low water

Mistflower
Conoclinium coelestinum
Full sun to partial shade
Will tolerate wide variety of water conditions

Weeping Lantana
Lantana montevidensis
Full sun
Moderate water

Firebush
Hamelia patens
Full sun to partial shade
Low water

Pogada Flower
Clerodendrum paniculatum
Full sun
Low water

Scarlet Milkweed
Asclepias curassavica
Full sun to partial shade
Low water

Butterfly Bush
Buddleia spp.
Full sun
Low water requirements

Jatropha
Jatropha integerrina
Full sun to partial shade
Low water

White Shrimp Plant
Justicia brandegeana
Full sun to partial shade
Low water

Mexican Sage
Salvia leucantha.
Full sun
Moderate water

Walter's Viburnum
Viburnum obovatum
Full sun
Moderate water

Tampa Vervain
Vervain spp.
Full sun
Low water

Mexican Flame Vine
Senecio confus
Full Sun
Low Water Requirements

Carolina Wild Petunia
Ruellian caroliniensis
Full sun/partial shade
Low water requirements

Spanish Needle
Coreopsis leavenworthii
Full sun/partial shade
Low water requirements

Raising Butterflies

COLLECTING BUTTERFLIES

The best way to find caterpillars is to look for plants that are known host plants for the butterflies in your area or plant your own host plants in containers or better yet plant a butterfly garden and wait for the females to lay their eggs on them, and they will!! A few common butterfly attracting plants are:

Milkweed to attract Monarchs and Queens
Bahama Cassia to attract Sulfur Butterflies (orange barred, cloudless and sleepy yellow)
Passion Vines (Suberosa and Incaranata) to attract Julias, Zebras and Gulf Fritillary

WHERE TO RAISE YOUR CATERPILLARS

I use Styrofoam coolers with an insert of screening in most of the top for sight and ventilation. Do not keep in direct sunlight. I put about 10 – 12 in each box, avoid overcrowding. Use as many coolers as you want.

FEEDING YOUR CATERPILLARS

This is the hard part...to provide enough fresh food cuttings from their host plants every day. Caterpillars will only eat the cuttings from their host plant, and will starve to death before they would eat the wrong food. Another way is providing a potted host plant in their box if it isn't too big.

KEEPING BOXES AND CATERPILLARS CLEAN
VERY IMPORTANT!!

Caterpillars have one job in life, that's eating. Because of this they have a lot of waste (known as frass). I clean our boxes using a 3" paint brush, brushing out the frass and debris every day and add fresh food. If you are using potted plants, put the new plant in the box and after a couple of hours the caterpillars will usually switch over to the next host plant. When cleaning, be sure not to throw out any caterpillars. Look carefully, it happens.

HANDLING CATERPILLARS

Caterpillars are susceptible to a lot of bacterial infections so handle as little as possible. Using a small paintbrush (model brush) helps to transfer them from box to box without any human contact. If a caterpillar is motionless for a time it is probably going through one of it's instars or it may be getting ready to form it's chrysalis so leave it alone.

CARING FOR YOUR CHRYSALIS

When they are ready caterpillars will stop eating. They will usually go to the top of the containers and pupate. I remove the chrysalis using a pin at the top of the chrysalis where the silk is, which is what they produce to secure themselves. Wrapping the silk around a pin, I put them in a separate container giving them enough room to expand their wings fully when exiting the chrysalis. It usually takes about ten days. If pupa has come loose from its silk it still can be glued at the tip to a pin for the same results. Misting the chrysalis is important to keep the humidity high. Every morning while feeding the caterpillars I watch the chrysalis. It only takes minutes for the butterfly to emerge and usually happens before 9am.

BUTTERFLIES EMERGE

It's best to wait a few hours after emergence until the wings have hardened to release the butterfly. It's a great feeling watching one of your friends you have raised fly away. If you have a butterfly garden of host and nectar plants, they will stay in your backyard. They usually stay within 200 yards of where they are raised provided you have enough nectar plants for them to feed on and host plants for them to lay their eggs on. Believe me this works. I've been doing it for years!!

Plastic Shoe box

Styrofoam cooler

Butterfly Gardening
with
Native Plants

n=nectar plants   h=host plants
(This is a partial list to get started)

Aster carolinianns	(Climbing Aster)	h-n
Sambucus simpsonii	(Elderberry)	n
Sophora tomentosa	(Necklace Pod)	n
Lantana involucrate	(White Wild Sage)	n
Salix caroliniana	(Coastal Plain Willow)	h
Phyla nodifloria	(Carpetweed)	h-n
Bacopa spp.	(Water Hyssop)	h-n
Boehmeria cylindrical	(False Nettle)	h
Borrichia spp.	(Oxeye Daisy)	n
Asclepias tuberose	(Butterfly Weed)	h-n
Conoclinium coelestinum	(Mist Flower)	n
Rivina humilis	(Rouge Plant)	n
Hypericum myrtiflollum	(Saint John's Wort)	n
Piloblephis rigida	(Penny Royal)	n
Coreopis leavenworthii	(Tickseed)	n
Helianthus debilis	(Beach Sunflower)	n
Mimosa strigillosa	(Sunshine Mimosa)	n
Lantana depressa	(Pineland Lantana)	n
Cordia globosa	(Bloodberry)	n
Erythrina herbacea	(Coral Bean)	n
Hamelia patens	(Firebush)	n

Gaillardia pulchella	(Blanket Flower)	n
Flaveria linearis	(Yellowtop)	n
Persea borbonia	(Red Bay)	h
Liquidambar styraciflua	(Sweet Gum)	h
Magnolia virginianna	(Sweet Bay Magnolia)	n
Vervain	(Tampa Vervain)	h
Passiflora incarnate	(Purple Passionflower)	h-n
Passiflora suberosa	(Corkey Stem Passionflower)	h-n
Heliotropum angiospermum	(Scorpion Tail)	n
Solidago sempervinens	(Seaside Goldenrod)	n
Bidens alba	(Spanish Needle)	h-n
Lonicera sempervinens	(Coral Honeysuckle)	n
Duranta repens	(Golden Dew Drop)	n
Ruellia succulenta	(Wild Petunia)	h-n
Viburnum obovatum	(Walter`s Viburnum)	n
Cassia ligustrina	(Privet Senna)	h-n
Stachytarpheta jamaicensis	(Blue Porterweed)	n
Lysiloma latisilgvum	(Wild Tamarind Tree)	n
Salvia coccinea	(Tropical Sage)	n
Psychotria nervosa	(Wild Coffee)	n
Zanthoxylom fagara	(Wild Lime)	h
Zamia floridana	(Coontie)	h
Jacquemontia vine	(Key's Morning Glory)	n
Lepidum virginicum	(Pepper Grass)	h
Fitharexylum fruticosum	(Fiddlewood)	n

Butterfly Nectar Plants

This is a partial list to get you started.

Ruby Red Pentas	*Pentas lanceolata*
Porter Weed	*Stachytarphaeta urticifloia*
Moss Verbena	*Glandularia pulchella*
Tropical Sage	*Salvia coccinea*
Mexican Sage	*Salvia leucantha*
Mexican Petunia	*Ruellia brittoniana*
Golden Dewdrop	*Duranta repens*
Blanket Flower	*Gaillardia pulchella*
Fire Bush	*Hamelia patens*
Butterfly Bush	*Buddleia davidii*
White Shrimp Plant	*Justicia brandegeana*
Tampa Verbain	*Glandularia tampensis*
African Bush Daisy	*Euryops* hybrid
Cigar Plant	*Cuphea micropetala*
Marigolds	*Tagetes spp.*
Tickseed	*Coreopsis spp.*
Jatropha	*Jatropha integerrima*
Bougainvillea	*Bougainvillea glabra*
Impatiens	*Impatiens wallerana*
Beach Sunflower	*Helianthus debilis*
Indigo Spires	*Salvia faranacea x longispicata*
Phlox	*Phlox spp.*
Philippine Violet	*Barleria cristata*
Zinnia	*Zinnia spp.*
Bloodberry	*Cordia globosa*
Blackeyed Susan	*Rudbeckia hirta*
Plumbago	*Plumbago ariculata*
Scorpion Tail	*Heliotropium angiospernum*
Purple Coneflower	*Echinacea purpurea*

Mist Flower	*Conoclinium coelestinum*
Lantana	*Lantana spp.*
Seaside Goldenrod	*Solidago sempervirens*
Scarlet Milkweed	*Asclepias curassavica*
Blazing Star	*Liatris spp.*
Spanish Needle	*Bidens pilosa*

Butterfly *and* Host Plants

Black Swallowtail
Parsley (*Ptilimnium capillaceum*)
Fennel (*Foeniculum vulgare*)
Dill (*Anethum graveolens*)

Zebra Longwing
Passion Vines
Maypop (*Passiflora incaranata*)
Corkey Stem (*Passiflora suberosa*)

Polydamas (Gold Rim)
Dutchman's Pipe
(*Aristolochia elegans*)
(*Aristolochia gigantean*)

White Peacock
Water Hyssop (*Bacopa monnieri*)
Frog Fruit (*Lippia nodifloria*)

Monarch
Milkweeds
Scarlet (*Asclepias curassavica*)
Giantica (*Asclepias ginantea*)
Swamp (*Asclepias perennis*)

Great Southern White
Pepper Grass (*Lepidium virginicum*)

Julia
Passion vines
Maypop (*Passiflora incaranata*)
Corkey Stem (*Passiflora suberosa*)

Gulf Fritillary
Passion Vines
Maypop (*Passifloria incaranata*)
Corkey Stem (*Passifloria suberosa*)

Cloudless Sulfur
Cassias (Senna)
Desert (*Cassia nemophila*)
Bahama (*Cassia bicapsularis*)
Candle Plant (*Cassia alata*)

Buckeye
Frogfruit (*Lippa nodiflora*)
Plantains

Queen
Milkweeds
Scarlet (*Asclepias curassavica*)

Orange Barred Sulfur
Cassias (*Senna* spp.)
Desert Cassia (*Senna nemophila*)
Bahama Cassia (*Senna bicapsularis*)
Candle Plant (*Cassia alata*)

Malachite
Green Shrimp Plant (*Justicia bendage*)
Mexican Petunia (*Ruellia brittionia*)

Painted Lady
Mallows (*Malva* ssp.)

Red Admiral

Nettles (*Boehmeria*)

Giant Swallowtail

Citrus
Wild Lime (*Zanthoxylum fagara*)

Cassius Blue

Plumbago (*Plumbago auriculata*)

Large Orange Sulfur

Cassias (*Senna* spp.)
Desert (*Cassia nemophila*)
Bahama (*Cassia bicapsularis*)
Tamarind Tree (*Lysiloma latisilgvum*)

Luna Moth

Sweet Gum (*Liquidambar styraciflua*)

Palamedes Swallowtail

Red Bay Tree (*Persea borbonia*)

Question Mark

American Elm (*Ulmas americana*)

Tiger Swallowtail

Sweet Bay Tree (*Magnolia virginiana*)

Sleepy Orange

Sicklepod (*Cassia obtusifolia*)
Coffeeweed (*Cassia occidentalis*)

Glossary

Abdomen:	Lower and third section of body
Chrysalis:	Cocoon-like structure formed by caterpillar where transformation into butterfly occurs.
Fore Wings:	Front or upper pair of wings on butterflies
Frass:	Caterpillar excrement
Head:	First of three parts of butterfly body; eyes, antennae are located on the head
Hind Wings:	Back or lower pair of wings on butterflies
Host Plants:	Plants female butterflies deposit eggs on
Instars:	Molting or skin-shedding stages of caterpillars
Larvae:	Second stage of complete metamorphosis caterpillars
Legs:	Used for holding on and tasting
Nectar Plants:	Plants adult butterflies feed on
Ocelli:	Eyespots on butterflies and moths
Osmeteria:	Horn-like protrusions on the head of the caterpillar. Osmeteria emit a foul odor which is used to intimidate predators.
Proboscis:	Coiled 'tongue' used to drink water and flower nectar.
Puddling:	Term used when butterflies gather on moist soil to sip water.
Pupa:	Third stage of complete metamorphosis where caterpillar forms the chrysalis.
Roost:	Place where butterflies rest at night
Scales:	Covering on hind and fore wings that provides the colors we see
Scent Pouches:	Spots on male butterfly hind wings
Thorax:	Second or mid section of body where wings are attached

Visit Public
Butterfly Gardens in Florida

Cypress Gardens Winter Haven, FL (800) 237-4826
Beautiful outdoor garden with an enclosed atrium; native and exotic butterflies.

Marie Selby Gardens Sarasota FL (941) 366-5731
Great outdoor butterfly garden.

Caribbean Gardens Goodlette Frank Rd., Naples FL (239) 262-5409 A good example of butterfly gardening with native and tropical Plants.

University of Florida Extension Service Collier County 14700 Immokalee Rd., Naples, FL (239) 353-7127
Beautiful outdoor walk-through butterfly garden plus many other gardens to tour.

Butterfly World 3600 W. Sample Rd., Trade Wind Park, Coconut Creek, FL (305) 977-4400
Great indoor and outdoor gardens, native and tropical Butterflies.

Briggs Nature Center 401 Shell Island Rd, Naples FL (239) 775-8569 Outdoor Butterfly Garden

Sugden Regional Park (239) 417-2003 E Tamiami Trail, Naples FL
Beautiful butterfly garden

May the left hand of God
rest gently
on all of those who are kind
to His many creatures
and may His other hand
deliver a thundering right hook
to those that are not.

-Larry Watson

Made in the USA
Charleston, SC
06 June 2013